Heal

Yourself

This book belongs to:

____

____

____

Copyright © 2022 by eaglespringsolotions publishers

Disclaimer

This book has been written for information purposes only. Every effort has been made to make this Book as complete and accurate as possible. However, there may be mistakes in typography or content. Also, this e-book provides information only up to the publishing date. Therefore, this Book should be used as a guide - not as the ultimate source. The purpose of this Book is to educate. The author and the publisher do not warrant that the information contained in this book is fully complete and shall not be responsible for any errors or omissions. The author and publisher shall have neither liability nor responsibility to any person or entity with respect to any loss or damage caused or alleged to be caused directly or indirectly by this book.

Table of Contents

Dedication……………………………………………7

Acknowledgment……………………………….8

Introduction…………………………………….9

Chapter 1 – Look at Mistakes as Lessons Instead of Regrets………………..……………………………13

Chapter 2 – Know Thy Self ……………………19

Chapter 3 – Know Thy Limitation ……………23

Chapter 4 – Be Truthful ……..…………………33

Chapter 5 – Be Considerate…………………….38

Chapter 6 – Be Tolerant.. ……………………….45

Chapter 7 – Be Generous ………………………58

Chapter 8 – Be Yourself……………………….64

Conclusion……………………………………….70

DEDICATION

This book is dedicated to my Wife and Children

ACKNOWLEDGEMENT

I want to appreciate my wife for her courage and support during the cause of putting the book together. And to my kids, Daddy loves you

Introduction

I'm so sick of all the bad vibes here! Do you? This world is unhealthy and polluted. I detest reading the newspaper, watching the news, and even talking to my neighbors. I don't want to seem like an outcast. I truly care about others. But this world has turned us into icy, ruthless people.

A society of dissatisfied individuals is the outcome. Divorce occurs in well over half of all marriages. Over half of all young individuals do not even think that marriage exists. We need to go back to the time when being nice was commonplace and it was simple to chat to strangers. Those were the days when neighbors watched out for one another and people genuinely believed in love. We must once more learn to love ourselves. The change we want to see in the world must start with each of us. We must begin to mend and love ourselves once more. People who are successful tend to be happy. Simply said, happiness makes it simple to stay motivated to accomplish your goals. Your ideas have a huge influence on the kind of life you lead and the relationships you will have with loved ones, friends, and romantic partners. Some people even contend that contemporary medicine cannot fully account for the impact that our ideas and beliefs might have on our health. Think about these instances: A middle-aged man passes away a day after his doctor gave him a cancer diagnosis, despite the fact that an autopsy showed the doctor made a mistake. Despite not really being pregnant, many women who are anxious to have a baby start to experience true pregnancy symptoms including cravings and a growth in the size of their breasts. Participants in clinical trials for new antidepressants who have depression start to feel better about themselves even if they were just given a placebo and not the genuine medication. Having said that, it has been empirically demonstrated that changing the way you think about yourself and the environment around you may significantly enhance your relationships, career, and health. This is far less expensive than hiring a divorce lawyer or paying for therapy sessions. The goal of this book is to assist you in healing yourself of all the wounds and the effects of the surrounding negativity. I promise that if you learn to escape the suffering of this world, the quality of your life will significantly increase going forward.

Chapter 1

Look At Mistakes as Lessons Instead of Regrets

"Don't waste a good mistake, learn from it" is *aimed at encouraging people to not live on regrets but rather learn from their mistakes, ''Robert Kiyosaki''*. These sentiments are supported by Albert Einstein who said that *if you have never made a mistake then you have never tried something new.* I mean, if you didn't fail, how would you know you were ill-prepared? Or if you did get that job, how would you know that your skills are a bit behind?

"I wish I had worked more in school; by now, I would have moved up several levels. If only I could go back in time and correct the errors that led to the failure of my company. She left and is now in the arms of another man since you didn't take her seriously. These are just a few examples of the regrets some of us are experiencing right now. You aren't where you wanted to be, that much is certain. You are getting close to 40 years old and yet haven't established yourself. However, this does not obligate you to continue to criticize your past shortcomings and errors. Additionally, you don't learn to walk by obeying regulations, as Richard Branson famously stated. You learn by doing and by falling over".

How you react to a mistake will influence how quickly you pick yourself up and go on. The error provides a window through which to better understand you. You can only learn how knowledgeable you are and how far you can go by making errors since theory and practice are very different. As Napoleon Hill once stated, "every difficulty, every failure, and every grief brings with it the seed of an equal or larger reward." this aids in your self-preparation.

Analyzing and re-analyzing your circumstance is better than admitting you made a mistake and continues. Living in regret is equivalent to being insane, which is described by Albert Einstein as doing the same thing over and expecting a different result. The fact is, if you're wise, you'll never make the same mistake twice. Would you continue operating a vehicle while intoxicated after being involved in a tragic collision? Would you operate your company hands-off if it failed because you relied too heavily on someone with poor judgment? Obviously not!

"Mistakes are inevitable if you live a long time. But if you recognize the errors and absorb the lessons from them, you'll improve as a person. It's not how something has affected you; it's how you deal with it. The most important thing is to never give up. Mr. Clinton This previous US president's statement illustrates the fact that everyone makes errors. The difference between the wise and the ordinary person is that the former accepts and learns from it while the latter will be absorbed in it and live in regret. This is well brought out through this popular quote by Winston Churchill, one of the founding fathers of the US "All men make mistakes, but only wise men learn from their mistakes". Mistakes should be viewed like stepping stones and an eye opener and not a barrier to success or happiness.

Yes you are living a life of regret. You are knee-deep in debt, your partner has issued you divorce papers, you just flanked your finals, your business is getting liquidated, or you are losing your home. However, nothing stays forever. Even the strongest storm eventually passes just like daylight eventually shines in the darkest of nights. Wipe your tears, dust yourself up, get up and face life. "Experience is simply the name we give our mistakes." - Oscar Wilde

And as I conclude, I would like to encourage you to press on and always fix your eyes on the goal.

Remember, Bill Gates, the world's richest man said "its fine to celebrate success but it is more important to heed the lessons of failure".

Chapter 2

Know Thy Self

"The more you know yourself, the more patience you have for what you see in others." - Erik Erikson. Knowing who you are is a very crucial aspect of healing yourself. How can you avoid a disaster if you are simply floating through life with no clear sense of what you stand for, and what you refuse to tolerate?

There is a reason why the ambitious small-town girl who moves to the big metropolis frequently finds herself in a depressing and, dare I say, precarious scenario. Consider the disgruntled Doctor as well, who is only a doctor because his parents insisted he must be the first doctor in his family. What about the mama's boy who is chosen at random and dates a girl he despises only to please his mother? These three have many characteristics. The proverb that states that any route will be the proper one if we do not know where we are heading provides an explanation for their situation. The saying "if we do not stand for anything, we will fall for anything" is far better. In other words, it will be simple for just about anyone to influence us into making a choice we will regret for the rest of our life if we do not understand ourselves, including our aims, desires, and aspirations. It will be one of the toughest things you have ever had to do to live down a decision you regret, especially if you have to deal with its repercussions every day. Living with the consequences of these decisions is a big factor in why so many individuals are so abrasive and cruel. I don't want you to live your life in this manner. We shall have the keys to unlock our own potential when we take the time to comprehend who we truly are and the nuances of our own personalities. If you do not understand what it involves, you cannot become your best self. You are more likely to choose a profession that you enjoy when you are aware of who you are. And when you are pursuing a job you are enthusiastic about, it is pretty simple to be motivated with a passion to do great things.

In addition, when you are at your best, you will look for the kind of friends and relationships that will make you happy and help you to be your best self. They will be able to relate to your way of thinking and may even share it. These are the folks who won't mock your ambitions or be envious of your achievement. You'll become nicer, happier, and, dare I say it, more successful if you're surrounded by kind, helpful individuals. People with a strong sense of self are frequently more determined and upbeat. Because they made wise decisions, these people have complete control over their lives. Where others perceive obstacles, they are more inclined to recognize opportunity. Additionally, when you appreciate what you do, productivity comes much more easily. Additionally, the fact that you like your job will offer you an advantage over the competition and you won't need other people's approval to motivate you. The joy of a task well done will motivate you to keep going. I am aware that these circumstances may appear perfect, where our decisions are not influenced by the wishes of our family and where we are all resilient enough to resist the pressure they will exert on us to choose a certain option. But trust me when I say that getting to know and fully understanding yourself will provide you access to chances you would not otherwise have seen coming. When you are certain of the choice that is best for you, it will be simpler for you to resist the demands from others around you. I'm not telling you to ignore your obligations to support your family; rather, I'm telling you to know who you are and to always be loyal to your identity. When you are not dragging the burden of a poor decision about with you for the rest of your life, you will be lot happier as a consequence and much simpler to love.

How to Discover Yourself

Even if it's simpler stated than done, it's not impossible. Start by conducting some impartial analysis. This does not include only asking others in your immediate vicinity what they think of you. They won't be as objective as you need them to be because of your contacts with them, whether they are constructive or destructive. Using a credible personality test is a preferable choice. A popular option is the Myers-Briggs personality type test. Which of the personality types described by this theory best characterizes you will be determined by this test. It has grown in popularity recently since you can use the results to find out what kind of environment you operate best in and even how you connect with other people. In addition, whether you like the outcomes or not, they frequently exhibit astonishing accuracy.

Another excellent choice are exams of career aptitude. These are made to make it easier for you to comprehend your skill set and how you may use it to choose the best vocation. Starting a job that you love can never be too late. Once you have a well-thought-out plan in place that will enable you to take care of your obligations while also pursuing a passion project, go for it. Money may be limited, and you may already be pressed for time, making it unlikely that you can act at this moment. However, I would advise you to keep getting ready. Continue picking up as much information as you can about that profession online or from those around you. This will put you in a position to seize an opportunity if it presents itself. When you take the time to get to know yourself, you can uncover some unfinished business and hidden wounds that you probably would have preferred to keep buried. Unfortunately, you have been displaying these wounds in your interactions with others every day. You could have become too soft or too cold to care about other people's feelings as a result of these wounds. Become the finest version of yourself now that you can see yourself clearly. Respect yourself. Above everything, stay loyal to who you are. Knowing your limitations is yet another critical ability to develop in order to survive in this chaotic planet. The following chapter will cover this.

Chapter 3

Know Thy Limitations

"A great man is always willing to be little." —
Ralph Waldo Emerson

A key aspect of the results of a Myers-Briggs Personality type test is the section which outlines your strengths and weakness. If we were a bit more aware of our limits, many of the mistakes and issues we run into may have been completely avoided. Just picture a weightlifter who is overly enthusiastic and attempts to lift too much too quickly. What do you anticipate happening? Any sane person will understand that the weightlifter will end up hurting themselves. Some would claim that this example promotes self-limitation, and if we do that and stop challenging ourselves, we will never realize our actual potential.

If you put your mind to anything, there are no limits to what you can do, and sometimes you won't know how powerful you are until you try. To attain your objectives, you must, however, make sure that reason and logic win over. Starting today with 20 pounds could be a better option if you have never lifted 100 pounds. There is nothing wrong with having a large picture perspective, but I would advise starting small and working your way up. I'm basically telling you to have realistic expectations. Being modest will not only prevent you from having high expectations, but it will also enable you to set reasonable deadlines for completing your tasks. When someone reaches a given age without having accomplished a certain objective, many individuals grow discouraged. But simply think about how different Mark Zuckerberg is from Colonel Sanders. Colonel Sanders didn't start Kentucky Fried Chicken (KFC) until he was 80 years old, whereas Mark Zuckerberg started his Facebook empire in his early 20s. Although both men are regarded as being tremendously successful, their success came at various eras. Perhaps you are simply not in the correct industry or it is simply not the proper moment for you. Choosing a job in a sector you are passionate about will help you maintain motivation and achieve success, as was discussed in chapter 1. These two males' lives provide as proof for this theory. Their zeal for what they loved led to their achievement.

You may avoid comparing your accomplishments to those of others by living a modest lifestyle. Others struggle to climb the ladder while others hit the ball out of the park on their first attempt. Some people get married as soon as they graduate from college, while others must wait a while and kiss a few frogs before they discover the proper match. In actuality, both Mark Zuckerberg and Colonel Sanders faced several obstacles in their own paths to success. And so will you. Do not anticipate a change in your life. No matter what you want to accomplish, you will have to work harder than you ever have and perhaps wait longer than you anticipated. Being humble has many attractive qualities that go well beyond accomplishment. This trait will prevent you from trying to chew off more than you can handle. Not every request needs to be accepted. This holds true for both your personal and professional lives. If you want to impress your boss, don't commit to unrealistic deadlines unless you are quite certain you can meet them. Do not be hesitant to seek for assistance if you have been assigned an assignment and are unclear how to complete it. Don't overcommit at your child's school if you have a family to support and a full-time job to attend to. Know your limitations. This holds true for your time, effort, feelings, and abilities. The following chapter will discuss how modesty goes hand in hand with honesty and how you may use it to better your life and cure yourself.

Chapter 4

Be Truthful

"Honesty is the fastest way to prevent a mistake from turning into a failure." - *James Altucher*

A thief is the only thing worse than a liar. Liars make life challenging and frequently are unaware of the extensive consequences of their conduct. Lying makes us miserable individuals because we have to continuously watch our backs and conceal our tracks. In actuality, few things are as poisonous as a liar. Never should we let the negative in this world drive us to deceive others. Your proximity to the cheating and stealing door will increase if you lie. Stop now while you're ahead. Just consider the potential results of one dishonest act:

❖ Loss of money.

- ❖ Loss of self-respect.

- ❖ Permanent harm to another person's reputation.

- ❖ Permanent harm to relationships.

- ❖ Permanent harm to your own reputation.

- ❖ Guilty feelings.

- ❖ Insomnia

- ❖ A lack of trust.

The words honor, sincerity, fairness, integrity, uprightness, virtue, and truthfulness can all be used as synonyms for the term honesty. It takes more than just not lying when things are tough to be honest. Being morally straight in all circumstances is a requirement for honesty. In other words, we shall make every effort to be genuine and earn the trust of people around us via our deeds. But being honest may be very difficult. It is challenging to enumerate every situation when honesty is required. If you're confused if anything you did was honest or not, a useful test is whether you had to conceal it or trick someone into thinking you did something else. You are probably not being honest if you feel the need to conceal your tracks after doing or saying anything. Any difficulties you may have as a result of this training pale in comparison to the advantages of being honest. Imagine the peace of mind it would provide you to not have to second-guess everything you do or continuously look over your shoulder for signs that you are being discovered. Imagine waking up each day with no crushing guilt attached to your deeds. And don't imagine that being honest serves no one's interests. Being drawn to and respecting an honest person is pretty simple. When looking for new employees or contemplating a potential promotion within their company, the majority of employers place the biggest value on that quality. Being truthful does not entail disclosing all of our private matters to everyone attempting to eavesdrop on our affairs. Instead, we should not withhold pertinent information from those who are entitled to an honest response. Being honest also entails resisting the numerous strategies that may emerge to obtain more than we merit or deceive others into thinking something untrue about us. However, there are instances when some of us could find ourselves in really disastrous situations as a result of being perceived as being too honest. When our remarks are not balanced with love, this is frequently the case. We'll look at how that quality helps prevent many of the issues that can arise from that kind of communication in the following chapter.

Chapter 5

Be Considerate

"Kindness is the language which the deaf can hear and the blind can see." - Mark Twain

Being nice entails being hospitable, thoughtful, compassionate, and friendly. You need to be a friend in order to make one. The proverb "birds of a feather, flock together" is even more overused. You need to be the type of person that attracts joyful, encouraging individuals into your life. If not, why would anyone want to be around you?

People will remember how they felt as a result of an interaction for a very long time, as the astute Maya Angelou pointed out. When we act cruelly, we make life more tougher than it needs to be for others around us. When we are nasty or unfriendly, we make people feel unwanted, undervalued, and alone. Would you want it to happen to you? Would you like being treated so harshly? Do you not believe that treating people that way at work, school, or even in your own home makes your life far more difficult than it needs to be?

Even when individuals don't know one other well, kindness encourages collaboration. It is far simpler to take on the world with the help of others than it is to attempt to do it on your own. Being cruel encompasses a wide range of behaviors. The most prevalent way we act rude is through our words. Being unfriendly can be seen as being rude, condescending, or even abrupt. In addition to being rude, speaking negatively of others while praising oneself is a very selfish conduct that frequently does more harm than good. Being courteous is a crucial component of compassion. Let's spend some time learning more about this lovely trait.

Why Be Courteous

It's not as difficult as some people make it out to be. Because of the unkind attitudes of those around us, it is true that being courteous is getting harder, yet it is still achievable. These people's egos may be inflated by our politeness, but it does not reflect poorly on them. Whatever the circumstance, being polite reflects favorably on our character. People who are courteous are frequently seen as being nice, upright, competent, and pleasant. And in this highly linked society, it's impossible to tell who you could have offended. Imagine how humiliated you would feel if you attended a job interview only to learn that the man you had just yelled at in the parking lot for parking in "your" place was really the interviewer. You may experience it; believe me, it has occurred many times before.

Respecting and taking into account the needs, feelings, time, resources, values, and cultural conventions of others is part of being courteous. Being kind and nice will make you very likeable and inspire others to show you the same courtesy. Being courteous will also make it quite simple for you to win the respect of others around you. They will be made to respect you and your values even if they do not immediately alter their conduct. They could eventually improve as a consequence of your efforts. If we all had employment where our coworkers, employees, and subordinates treated us with respect, wouldn't life be lot simpler? Being nice is one of the simplest ways to garner respect, which must be earned.

Rules for Courtesy and Kindness

1. Don't say, post, or even think anything unkind if you don't have anything kind to say about it. Even whispered remarks to a buddy have been known to come back to harm the speaker.

2. Be generous with your salutations and greets. If you go into a room, give everyone a warm welcome. Please excuse yourself as you depart. And if someone greets you, give them a nice grin in return.

3. Don't belittle other people's efforts, especially when it's clear that they worked really hard to complete a task. If you must, follow up any constructive criticism with an actual compliment.

4. Show gratitude for other people's efforts. There is no need to express your disapproval if what is offered doesn't suit you.

5. Try to gain some insight into the cultural mores and viewpoints of individuals who are close to you. You only need to be informed enough to avoid accidentally offending someone; you do not have to agree with their viewpoints. Allowing people to openly voice these opinions without worrying about being insulted is also the politest thing to do. You can always come to an understanding.

6. You don't have to always demand that things be done your way. Every once in a while, let someone else to shine.

7. Avoid dominating discussions by talking exclusively about yourself and your achievements. Asking about oneself and paying attention to what they have to say demonstrates a genuine interest in the other person.

8. Pay close attention to what others are saying while they are speaking to you. Make eye contact and stop moving or typing or doing anything else. When someone interrupts you gently because you are busy, take a moment to consider how long the discussion should last, let them know you value what they have to say, and then set up a more convenient time to continue.

Chapter 6

Be Tolerant

"The weak can never forgive. Forgiveness is the attribute of the strong."- Gandhi

Forgiveness is not always simple. The simple fact that we need to use the phrase suggests that we have suffered some sort of harm. One of the biggest presents you can offer yourself is to forgive a grudge, whether it be genuine or imagined. Whether or whether you think the person deserves such generosity, this is true. We develop resentment when we refuse to forgive. It's like swallowing poison and expecting the person who hurt us to die when we hold onto hatred. It's comparable to causing injuries to our own body and expecting someone else to experience the anguish. This reasoning is not just flawed but also highly perilous. Hatred is a highly unpleasant emotion that may quickly develop from resentment. But why is it so difficult for us to forgive? Why does the thought of letting go of the pain make us feel so uneasy if forgiving someone who has injured us can be so beneficial?

The actual issue is that none of us want to keep going through the agony of whatever evil was done to us. However, when we continue to reflect on how much we were harmed, we unintentionally start to consider holding the offender accountable. Our faulty sense of justice frequently leads us to think that we will receive the justice we deserve if we hang on to every bit of suffering that was brought on and refuse to let it go. This is especially true if the offender doesn't seem to regret their actions. Unfortunately, refusing them our friendship or goodwill out of resentment will not make the person change for the better. By forcing our thoughts to repeatedly experience the agony, we are just doing ourselves harm.

Our appearance, our words, and our attitude will all suffer as a result of the heavy weight of anger that weighs heavily on our emotions as we storm violently through life.

Even if we could have just been harmed by one or a few people, everyone around us will start to feel the effects. We are frequently agitated, sad, and otherwise highly unpleasant when we are resentful. And to make matters worse, the individuals who suffer as a result of what happened are frequently the people we love rather than the ones who offended us. Additionally, it has been shown that the burden of resentment has an impact on our memory, productivity at work, capacity for everyday chores, ability to concentrate, and even our desire for sex. Immune system deterioration, poor heart health, and even high blood pressure have all been connected to being resentful and reluctant to forgive. As you can see, holding onto grudges will never serve you well. But what is forgiveness exactly? Is it only a forgetfulness of what happened? Does accepting forgiveness include acting as if nothing happened? Nope. It's not that easy. When we forgive, we must go beyond just saying it.

We need to alter our attitudes about the person. It seems as though we are giving them a fresh start from scratch. You are not going to stand by while the circumstances harm you or the other persons involved. High emotional intelligence, self-control, and love are needed for this. Not only does forgiveness "get them off the hook" for what they did, but it also frees individuals involved to put the past behind them and focus on the present.

"Forgiveness means that you fill yourself with love, and you radiate that love outward. You need to refuse to hang onto the venom or hatred that was engendered by the behaviors that caused the wounds." - Wayne Dyer

Giving someone the power to control your happiness by allowing yourself to get that furious in response to their acts and to dwell on what happened for a protracted length of time. It feels as though you are letting them rule you, and they will keep doing so until you find the strength to forgive them. Another reason forgiveness is advantageous is because it frequently follows self-awareness. When we keep in mind that we too have frequently had to seek for forgiveness, forgiving others becomes simpler for us. Despite what we might think, we are not flawless. Sometimes, without even realizing it, we injure those around us—even the ones we love. It will be simple for people close to us to forgive us when we make mistakes if we choose not to hold grudges and actively practice forgiveness. Several benefits of forgiving others include the following:

❖ You will be a lot happier and in a much better mood

❖ You will sleep better at night

❖ You will not jeopardize your job by not being productive

❖ You will not jeopardize your relationship with your significant other or your family

❖ You will learn greater self-control and self-awareness

❖ Your will enjoy greater peace

❖ You will gain the respect of those around you26

❖ You will no longer feel the pain of the damage that was done

❖ You will experience less anxiety

❖ Your self-esteem will increase as you observe your own personal strength

What Forgiveness is Not!

Being forgiving does not need you to be a pushover who continually allows themselves to be wounded. While you will absolutely let go of whatever resentment you may have against the offending person or parties, you do not have to put yourself in a situation where you may experience the same type of harm. After seeing what these individuals are capable of, it is quite reasonable to exercise a bit extra caution. But please, proceed with caution. Don't fall into the trap of believing that a person's actions speak for who they are when they commit minor infractions, which are ones that weren't done with malice aforethought. Please keep in mind that we are all human and have all hurt someone. Retaliation is not a possibility after forgiveness. It is not a declaration that you now have the "upper hand" to say you have forgiven someone. Even if the parties involved may have been at fault, they have no obligation to you. By making this peace offering and letting go of the anger that formerly engulfed you, you have gained a lot, even if they do not apologize. Keep in mind that by being forgiving, you are benefiting yourself. Although they could gain from your choice, you are actually offering yourself a gift by forgiving them.

How to Forgive

I would never expect that you forgive someone who has wronged you instantaneously or all at once since we both know that doing so is difficult. You have the choice to provide forgiveness gradually. By gradually letting go of your animosity against those who have harmed you, you will give yourself enough time to purge all traces of your bitterness from your mind and heart.

If you frequently have the chance to interact with this individual, you might begin by just saying hello. They could be taken aback by this since they did not anticipate such a thoughtful act, which could pave the door for the conversation you two need to reach a resolution. It is often preferable to take the effort to make things right even when you were wronged. Regardless of whether they appreciate the gesture or not, always keep in mind how this modest action will benefit you in the long term.

Writing down the name of the person or people who wounded you and making a list of everything they have ever done to irritate you is another easy activity that will enable us to forgive. Once you've finished that list, make a list of all the times you've offended someone and needed their forgiveness. We don't usually think about things like these Having a clear understanding of how frequently we have caused harm to individuals close to us, especially to those we love, may be the motivation we need to forgive. Some people find it even more unsettling to read the names of the people they dislike on the list of people they have had to seek for forgiveness from.

Making a list of all the nice things this individual has done for you might be another fruitful activity. This activity can help you keep in mind that despite their flaws, this person or those people also possess a lot of lovely traits. These characteristics, in the case of people closest to us, are the same reasons we loved them and initially held them near. Just consider: by offering an olive branch of peace, you may be able to persuade that individual to see the error of their ways and make a positive change. If you had even helped one person improve their character, the world would be a better place. Such generosity is not unappreciated or unrewarded. To be forgiving, one must be very resilient. But consider how much better our lives would be if we did not go through each day carrying bitterness and anger. One of the finest ways to cure ourselves is to release that oppressive load. This planet is already in a terrible state, and increasing animosity would only make matters worse. The next chapter will discuss how being kind may help us become more happier and more successful persons in this world.

Chapter 7

Be Generous

"If you can't feed a hundred people, then just feed one." —Mother Teresa

It is not necessary for a generous person to give away everything they own. A charitable person is also not compelled to put up with being used as a punching bag. First and foremost, being generous is being willing to give more than is necessary or being ready to offer.

Generosity elevates kindness to a new level. Even though you have a good heart and frequently consider ways to help others, you have not completely mastered the art of generosity until you take the initiative to start volunteering your time, effort, or other resources for the benefit of another person.

We are motivated by generosity to give of oneself voluntarily without expecting anything in return.

I understand that you might be questioning how donating your possessions can improve your quality of life. The reality is that a lot of people think that being kind is one of the secrets to finding true happiness in this wretched world. Actually, a lot of doctors will witness to the fact that being kind is excellent for your health. In reality, the following are some certain advantages of generous giving:

- ❖ Reduced stress

- ❖ Lessening the likelihood of suffering from depression

❖ Increased sense of purpose

❖ Greater happiness

❖ Stronger families and marriages

❖ Less clutter

❖ Reduced risk of dementia

❖ Greater appreciation for all that you have

❖ More likely to benefit from the generosity of others

A generous individual frequently looks for chances to help others. Consider the volunteers who travel to soup kitchens every weekend to provide a hand. We who had the guts to join the Peace Corps are also thought to be pretty kind. However, even a small act of generosity, such as pausing to let a youngster cross the street or helping an old woman with her shopping bags, might be regarded as kind.

This type of care for others is advantageous because it compels us to concentrate on their needs rather than our own issues. Anything that lessens the impact of our issues, whether they be interpersonal or financial, will have an immediate impact on our health. Being generous shields us from the cynicism and narcissism that make navigating this world so challenging. However, I would advise you to use caution as you try to be more giving. Pay close attention to how you show others your kindness. Please exercise extra caution when giving to those of the opposing sex. If you're already in a relationship and don't want to give the incorrect impression, stay away from favors or presents that are too intimate. Anything involving one's body is considered a personal gift. For instance, perfume would be seen as a personal present.

Please keep in mind that being generous may compromise your personal safety. When requested for money by a person who appeared to be destitute, many individuals have been robbed. No matter how desperate the individual seems to be, it's never a good idea to go into your wallet or purse and show where and how much cash you have. Telling the person you'll be back with a present is a safer course of action. I would highly advise that you pack up everything that you would like to gift to this person in advance and travel to a safe place that is away from inquisitive eyes. The last bit of advice I have is to be cautious before being overly kind. Some individuals enjoy spontaneity, while others would rather you first inquire whether they need your assistance. Even the finest intentions might backfire on you if they are not carried out properly. We've talked at length about how developing different facets of your personality may aid in your self-healing and prevent you from carrying around a lot of the emotional baggage that comes with the negativity in this world. The final of this book holds the most important key to healing all the scars caused by this nasty world. Please read on to learn more about what that is.

Chapter 8

Be Yourself

"Be yourself; everyone else is already taken." — *Oscar Wilde*

"The greatest gift you ever give is your honest self." — *Fred Rogers*

We all need to rediscover who we are. This is one of the most important components of surviving this tragedy we call life. This support does not in any way grant you license to do badly. We've previously spoken about how we must work hard to overcome our unfavorable characteristics in order to be able to cure ourselves from the suffering this world has created.

Character flaws like haughtiness, rudeness, arrogance, and stinginess have no place in your life. We open the door to all kinds of negativity when we proudly carry these repulsive behaviors. That simply leads to greater suffering and disappointment. That's why I advised you in the first chapter to familiarize yourself with. By knowing more about your shortcomings, you will be more equipped to cure yourself.

What does it mean to be oneself exactly then? You must remove yourself from all the labels that the people around you have placed on you. These demeaning labels are a result of the way we seem, how we dress, or even the neighborhood where we were raised.

We have no justification for allowing the environment to shape us into a kind that doesn't accurately reflect who we are. Imagine how freeing it would be to not have to put on a false persona. Of course, everything here is reasonable. We would never wish to exercise some freedoms that may have a significant impact on our personal lives and perhaps put our employment in danger. Consequently, you might want to wait before making any major decisions, such as dyeing your hair purple and green, until you find a job that would allow you to make such a decision.

Here are the top 5 reasons you should start living authentically:

1. It is impossible to win over everyone. If you continuously let the people around you define who you are, you'll always need to modify your values in an effort to appease everyone. The only issue with this is that

you will have to juggle so many competing expectations that you will inevitably let someone down. Additionally, you won't be content with the results if you put yourself under this type of strain.

2. The civilization that surrounds us is genuinely apathetic. Both the submissive housewife and the tenacious achiever are portrayed in the media as the perfect woman. Men must also be considerate of the requirements of the other sex as well as the hazardous bad boy, according to society. Which one will you be if you only let those around you define who you are? Whatever you want to be, keep in mind that putting up this type of show every day is quite taxing.

3. You'll wind up making decisions that will alter your life dependent on the whims of those close to you; they won't be affected by the results of your actions. You will be the one who will have to take care of the child if you decide to have one just because your family feels it's time! If you choose a job because your friends and family think you'll succeed in it, you'll be stuck with it for the rest of your life.

4. The reality always comes to light. People will eventually figure out that you are lying. Unfortunately, the truth frequently comes out in a significant scandal or collapse, as we witness in the cases of many celebrities.

5. You will be genuinely happy when you are satisfied with who you are. When you are continuously trying to be someone you are not, how can you ever love yourself? All things considered, if you want to experience true progress, you must assume control over your life. If you are not courageous enough to make significant changes, you cannot expect different outcomes. And the moment has come for such adjustments!

Conclusion

I hope this book has been useful to you. I hope you have decided to make some much-needed improvements as a result of the benefit. Although progress could be gradual at first, you won't ever regret choosing to better yourself. Every action, no matter how tiny, counts as progress because it moves us closer to our goals. The good in us is rewarded by the universe, and it also assists us in seeing the good in others. You should be aware at this point that we hold the key to our own recovery and to surviving the tragedy that is life. Our lives won't become any better until we accept the mistakes we've made and actively attempt to fix them.

"As human beings, our greatness lies not so much in being able to remake the world - that is the myth of the atomic age - as in being able to remake ourselves." — Mahatma Gandhi